The Story of the

CONESTOGA WAGON

By Kenneth Richards

Illustrations by James G. Temple

CHILDRENS PRESS, CHICAGO

 Printed in the U.S.A.
Published simultaneously in Canada

Library of Congress Catalog Card Number 70-100700

4 5 6 7 8 9 10 11 12 13 14 15 16 17 18 19 20 21 22 23 24 25 R 75

A tired rider slumped in the saddle as he rode into the Conestoga Valley of Pennsylvania. He had come fifty miles overland from Philadelphia, leading a pack train.

"He's come! He's come!" the word spread quickly and happy farmers came to help with the packs and to care for the tired animals.

There were tools and tea, and sugar and cloth.

"Oh but we need so much more!" cried the farmers. "If you had a wagon, you could bring so much more."

"With a wagon, we could send grain to the city," said one of the men. "Now we have more than we need."

The pack train driver snorted. "A wagon! A lot of good a wagon would be on that trail. The wheels would sink in the mud. The trail goes almost straight up in places. Everything would slide out the back end. And it would take six horses to pull it, loaded."

"Are we not wagon builders from Germany?" said one of the farmers. "We will build a wagon for such a trail." And they did. It came to be known as the Conestoga wagon.

The Conestogas had a design that set them apart from other wagons in history. The body of the wagon, called a "bed" or "box", was curved upward at the ends. The front panel and tailgate were slanted like the bow and stern of a ship. A huge white cloth or canvas covered the whole wagon. Arched wooden bows held the cover which extended over both the front and the rear of the wagon bed.

There were many practical reasons for the Conestoga's unique features. The curved floor was designed to prevent the load from shifting backward or forward as the wagon rolled up or down steep hills. Since it was a three or four day trip between Lancaster and Philadelphia the cargo had to be protected from the weather. Some wagon owners purchased sail cloth on the docks in Philadelphia to make covers for their wagons. Others used hand-woven cloth from the Susquehanna Valley.

The Conestoga wagons did not have a driver's seat. The driver generally walked along beside the wagon on the left side. Sometimes he rode in a saddle on the rear left horse of the team. He held only one rein, or "jerk-line", and that was to the front left horse only.

As the driver controlled this lead horse, the rest of the team followed. When the lead horse turned, the team turned. Of course, like most harness horses, the team understood that "Giddap" meant "go" and "Whoa!" meant to stop, that "Gee" meant to turn right and "Haw" meant to turn left.

Not only were the Conestogas large, they were also colorful. The covers, of course, were always white. The outside of the wagon bed was usually painted blue and the running gear—that is, the wheels, axles, and brake assembly—were painted red.

The Conestogas were first seen traveling along the winding dirt wagon path that served as a road between Lancaster and Philadelphia. They carried crops grown in the Conestoga and Susquehanna valleys to the city. They also carried furs that had been taken in the mountains west of Lancaster.

On the return journey, tools, clothes, and other items manufactured in Europe or Philadelphia were carried to the inland farmers. Conestogas also served as farm wagons, used for daily chores on the valley farms.

The fame of the Conestoga wagons spread quickly through the colonies of America. In the South, owners of big plantations used them to haul tobacco to Charleston and Norfolk. Merchants in the Middle Colonies needed wagons to haul goods to the frontier

—or at least as far as the wagon trails went. New England farmers had to have wagons to move fruit and vegetables to Boston or Hartford and other cities.

"Build me a wagon like the Conestoga!" soon became the cry most heard by wagon builders from Massachusetts to Georgia.

In a few years, copies of the wagons were being produced in several of the colonies. But the name "Conestoga" remained—no matter where they were built.

One day in the spring of 1755, Thomas Pickerill stopped his Conestoga wagon in his yard and hurried into the kitchen of his farmhouse. Mrs. Pickerill was surprised to see him home from Lancaster so early.

"This is an advertisement signed by Benjamin Franklin," Mr. Pickerill said, waving a piece of paper. "It states that General Braddock, who commands the English army here in America, wants to hire wagons, teams, and drivers. War is brewing with the French and Indians to the west and Braddock needs wagons to haul his army's supplies. The pay is good and I am going to hire on."

Mrs. Pickerill was worried. "What will happen if our wagon is damaged or our horses are killed?" she asked. "If there is a battle, you may be injured too," she added.

"The English will pay for any losses," Mr. Pickerill

assured his wife. "And the army always protects its supply train. I will not be hurt."

Mrs. Pickerill knew there was no use arguing once her husband had made up his mind. Early the next morning he kissed his wife and children good-bye, and drove away with the big, white-covered Conestoga wagon pulled by their six great farm horses. Other wagons could be seen rolling slowly along the road leading south to Maryland where General Braddock and his army waited.

When he arrived at Wills Creek, Mr. Pickerill found nearly two-hundred other wagons parked in nearby fields and along the roads. An English army officer told him where to report and he soon learned

why General Braddock wanted all these wagons.

"We are going to drive the French out of Fort Duquesne over on the Ohio River," said one of the colonial soldiers serving with the English.

"But there aren't any roads over the Alleghenies," said a wagon driver. "How does General Braddock expect us to get these big Conestogas over the mountains and through the forests?"

"We are going to send a few hundred men ahead to cut a road," said the soldier. "It will be slow work, but it has to be done. The French can carry their supplies by boat on the St. Lawrence River and the Great Lakes. We have no other way except by wagon."

"I heard that Colonel Washington wanted to use pack horses," said one of the drivers.

"Yes," replied the soldier, "but that would mean leaving much of our equipment behind. General Braddock says we will need it all, and the only way to carry it is with your big wagons."

Several days went by as men worked hard to get all the wagons loaded. Some carried gunpowder and cannonballs. Others carried food for the men and horses. A few were loaded with clothing and medical supplies. At last, the expedition was ready to start.

Woodsmen had gone ahead to cut a road through the forests and over the mountains. They were several miles ahead of the wagon train. The road they built was not a very good one and progress was slow. Often the wagons made only two or three miles in a day. It was hard work and required great skill to guide the big wagons over the narrow road.

Day after day, mile after mile, Mr. Pickerill and the other drivers urged their teams along the rough mountain road. They passed wagons with broken wheels or axles. The brakes on the Conestogas did not help much when the steep road plunged down a mountain. The drivers chained the rear wheels so they would not roll and then they very carefully skidded the wagon down. Some wagons tipped, and toppled off the narrow mountain road and were

smashed to pieces in the valley below.

After several weeks, General Braddock's army was within ten miles of Fort Duquesne. All during the long, tedious journey, Indian scouts had watched and kept the French informed as to how close the English army was getting. On July 9, 1755, the French and their Indian allies made a surprise attack upon Braddock's men.

The English troops, in their bright scarlet uniforms, were unused to fighting in the wilderness. The French and Indians, hidden behind rocks and trees in the forest, found the British easy targets. The colonial troops under Colonel Washington took cover and fought as the French and Indians did. The brave British troops stood shoulder to shoulder in a clearing and fired at their unseen enemy—but it was an uneven fight. At last, after General Braddock was mortally wounded, the British troops began to retreat. The colonials fought a rearguard action as the retreat quickly became a rout.

Thomas Pickerill heard the sounds of the fighting ahead, and he and all the other drivers halted their teams to await the outcome.

Suddenly, frightened British troops came scrambling down the road. "All is lost!" they shouted. "Run! Run for your lives!" Many drivers became frightened and unharnessed one horse of their team

and rode off pell-mell back down the wilderness road toward Maryland.

As Washington's colonials fought to slow the advancing French and Indians, Thomas Pickerill turned his team and wagon around. He would not leave his big Conestoga and six fine horses to the French. Driving his team as fast as he could, Pickerill moved carefully back down the road past abandoned wagons and frightened horses. Some other drivers were just as determined to save their wagons and soon a long line of Conestogas was moving eastward. Many days later they reached the safety of the fort at Wills Creek.

The expedition, which cost the life of General Braddock, was a failure. The British had met with a bad defeat. But a great contribution had been made to American life. Several years would pass before people would realize how much "Braddock's Road" would mean to America. It was the first road west through the mountains to the Ohio River Valley, and it opened a way for settlers to broad new lands.

The French eventually were defeated and lost all claim to this land. Fort Duquesne became Fort Pitt, and later the city of Pittsburgh. By 1770 hundreds of Conestogas were carrying settlers over Braddock's Road to a new life in the west.

Years passed and more roads were cut through the

Alleghenies. They were no better than Braddock's Road, however, and the big, tough Conestoga was still the best wagon in the country to travel these roads.

For many years, there were only dirt roads in America. Road building had to be done by hand with shovels, crowbars, hoes, axes and rakes. Usually the roads followed old Indian trails and horse paths. Trees were cut down to widen the paths. Big stones were removed and the roadbed was leveled and graded. Sometimes logs were cut and laid side by side to form what was called a "corduroy road." One can imagine how rough it must have been to ride along a corduroy road. The teams moved very slowly over them—but at least the logs kept wagons and stagecoaches from becoming stuck in mud.

Twenty years after Braddock's defeat, the American Revolutionary War began. Once again Conestogas were called upon to help in the struggle. They carried supplies for the American army and brought food to General Washington's starving soldiers at Valley Forge. The British surrendered at Yorktown, Virginia, in October of 1782. Americans had won their independence and Conestoga wagons had done their share.

Soon after the end of the Revolutionary War, people in the new nation began to clamor for better roads. But the war for independence had been costly. Neither the states nor the new federal government had any money for roads. In Pennsylvania, however, the state legislature encouraged private citizens to join the Philadelphia and Lancaster Turnpike Company. Many people invested their own money to build a two-lane highway which was begun in 1792 and completed in 1794 while George Washington was President of the new United States. It was the first of many similar highways to be built in America in the years that followed.

The Lancaster Turnpike was the first macadamized road in America. A Scotsman named John L. McAdam had designed and built this kind of road in Britain. The base, or roadbed, was made of graded earth with several inches of broken rock rolled on top of the earth. Then asphalt, tar, or oil was added to make a fairly smooth surface. Compared to unsurfaced dirt roads, the turnpike was like a ribbon of velvet!

The turnpike company charged travelers a fee. (Just so, turnpikes and great bridges are paid for by tolls today.) Tollgates were set up about every ten miles and every traveler had to stop and pay a fee before proceeding farther. A Conestoga wagon with four horses was charged about forty cents at each of these tollgates.

The tollgates usually consisted of a little gatekeeper's house, sometimes with a roof that extended across the turnpike. At some, the gatekeeper's wife sold food to the travelers. Some tollgates even had a waiting room where weary travelers could rest before going on their way.

A few travelers complained that it cost too much to travel on the turnpike.

"It costs me more than four dollars in tolls to make a round trip to Philadelphia," said one Lancaster farmer. "That is a lot of money for some of us poor farmers."

"Yes, but it may be a savings in the long run," replied another. "Our animals will live longer because it is easier to pull a wagon on a smooth road. Also, our wagons will not need repairs as often. My wagon used to break down or get stuck on nearly every trip I made on the old roads. Now we can roll right along to the city in a lot less time, too!"

As more and more roads stretched across eastern America, more Conestogas were needed to carry freight. Early in the 19th century, a plan was approved by congress to build a road over the old route cut by General Braddock fifty years before. This stretch of road from Cumberland, Maryland, across the Alleghenies to Wheeling, in what is now West Virginia, was completed in 1818. It was called the

National Road. It ushered in the greatest era for the Conestoga wagon.

Thousands of adventurous American settlers and pioneers had freedom to push westward through the barrier of the mountains to the rich prairie lands of Ohio, Indiana, Illinois, and the Missouri River Valley. With them went the great Conestoga wagons carrying all their possessions. At Wheeling and Pittsburgh some people took to the river boats and sailed down the Ohio River. Others drove their wagons on across the prairies of Indiana and Illinois to the Mississippi River and beyond.

One day a man stood on a hill and watched a long line of Conestogas rolling westward. They rocked and swayed like ships at sea, and their great white covers looked like sails. "They looked like the schooners I've seen sailing in and out of Boston harbor," the man said later. "Yes, that's what they are — *Prairie Schooners!*" It became a common nickname for the Conestogas and other covered wagons to follow.

As the roads improved, men began to build larger Conestogas. The biggest wagons weighed over three-thousand pounds and could haul three or four tons of freight. They stood ten-feet tall and the rear wheels were as high as a man. From end to end they measured over twenty feet. They were the largest land vehicles in America at the time.

Traffic along the western roads increased year by year. An almost endless stream of Conestoga wagons and Concord stagecoaches rocked and creaked over the mountain passes and across the rolling prairies. To serve the stagecoach passengers and the wagon drivers, many wayside inns sprang up. They were located about twelve to fifteen miles apart along the busy highways. The distance represented about a day's travel for a Conestoga. The inns sported such fancy names as The Fox, The Scarlet Cloak, The Green Tree, or The Two Swans. Drivers and passengers alike looked forward to the warmth, good food and rest at the wayside inns.

In the late afternoon, Conestogas began swinging into the wagon park of a roadside tavern. Every Conestoga had a feedbox attached to the rear of the wagon bed that was specially designed to fit on the wagon tongue. When the wagon was parked, the driver would unhitch the team, move the feedbox to the wagon tongue and fill it with fodder or grain. Three horses were then placed on each side of the tongue facing one another and all six horses could eat at the same time. Of course some Conestoga teams consisted of only five or four horses.

When the horses were fed, blankets were placed over them in cold weather and they were turned into a fenced corral behind the tavern. Only after the

TRAVELERS INN
& BLACKSMITH

horses were cared for did a driver go into the inn for food and rest.

There was a warm and friendly atmosphere in the old roadside inns. Most wagons were parked by early evening and, when all the drivers were ready, a big, hearty meal was served at long, rough tables. There were laughter, jokes, and storytelling, during the meal and afterwards, as the men sat around smoking their pipes. Most of the drivers were interested in where the others were headed.

"I'm heading for Terra Haute, Indiana, with a load of farm tools and kegs of nails for a general store," said one man.

"I've got a load of furniture from a store in Philadelphia," said another. "It's going to a family out in Vandalia, Illinois."

Of course the talk usually got around to the freight business in general as the evening wore on.

"Business has slowed down a lot since they opened that Erie Canal a few years ago," commented one man. "They can ship things that way faster and cheaper than we can."

"Yes," replied another, "but goods still have to go by wagon to the inland cities and towns. We will have plenty of business for years to come."

As the evening wore on, talk gradually faded as the drivers turned in to their bedrolls. They did not

take rooms at the inn. On warm nights in the summer they often slept out under the stars.

In the morning they were up before dawn, tending to their animals by the light of a lantern. After a hearty breakfast in the tavern, they swung their big Conestogas, one by one, out into the traffic of the National Road. The sun's first rays found them, harness bells jingling and wheels creaking, helping to move America westward.

Conditions were changing rapidly in America. Steamboats now plied the great western rivers. After the success of the Erie Canal, that extended across New York State from the Hudson River to Lake Erie, new canals were being built in many parts of the nation. By 1850, nearly three thousand miles of canals were in operation. All of this water traffic hurt the freight-wagon business.

"I'm worried about these new steam engines for the railroads," said one man. "I hear one of those engines can pull as much as ten Conestogas. They are building a railroad through the mountains now. Once they are through they will get all of the long-distance freight business."

A relatively new industry in America already was putting an end to the Conestoga wagon and the usefulness of the canals. This, of course, was the steam locomotive and the railroads. In 1830 there were only thirty miles of railroad track in the whole United States. By 1840 there were nearly three thousand miles and by 1850 over ten-thousand miles of track sprawled in every direction across eastern America. In 1852, the rails reached through the Allegheny Mountains to Pittsburgh. By 1855, one could travel all the way from New York to St. Louis, Missouri, on a train. The day of the Conestoga wagon was over.

There were still hundreds of Conestogas being used in places where there was no canal or railroad. Hundreds of others were used for many more years as farm wagons. Some of the old Conestogas led the way across the plains of the far west along the Santa Fe Trail. A few made the torturous journey over the Oregon Trail and across the Sierra Nevada Mountains to California. But no new Conestoga wagons were being built.

Thousands of covered wagons carried pioneers across Kansas, Colorado, and Nevada to the Pacific coast, of course, but these were not Conestogas. Most of them had basically the same running gear and similar white cloth covers. But here the similarity ended.

The covered wagons that pushed the frontier westward from the Mississippi and Missouri rivers were lighter than the Conestogas. Their wagon bed was

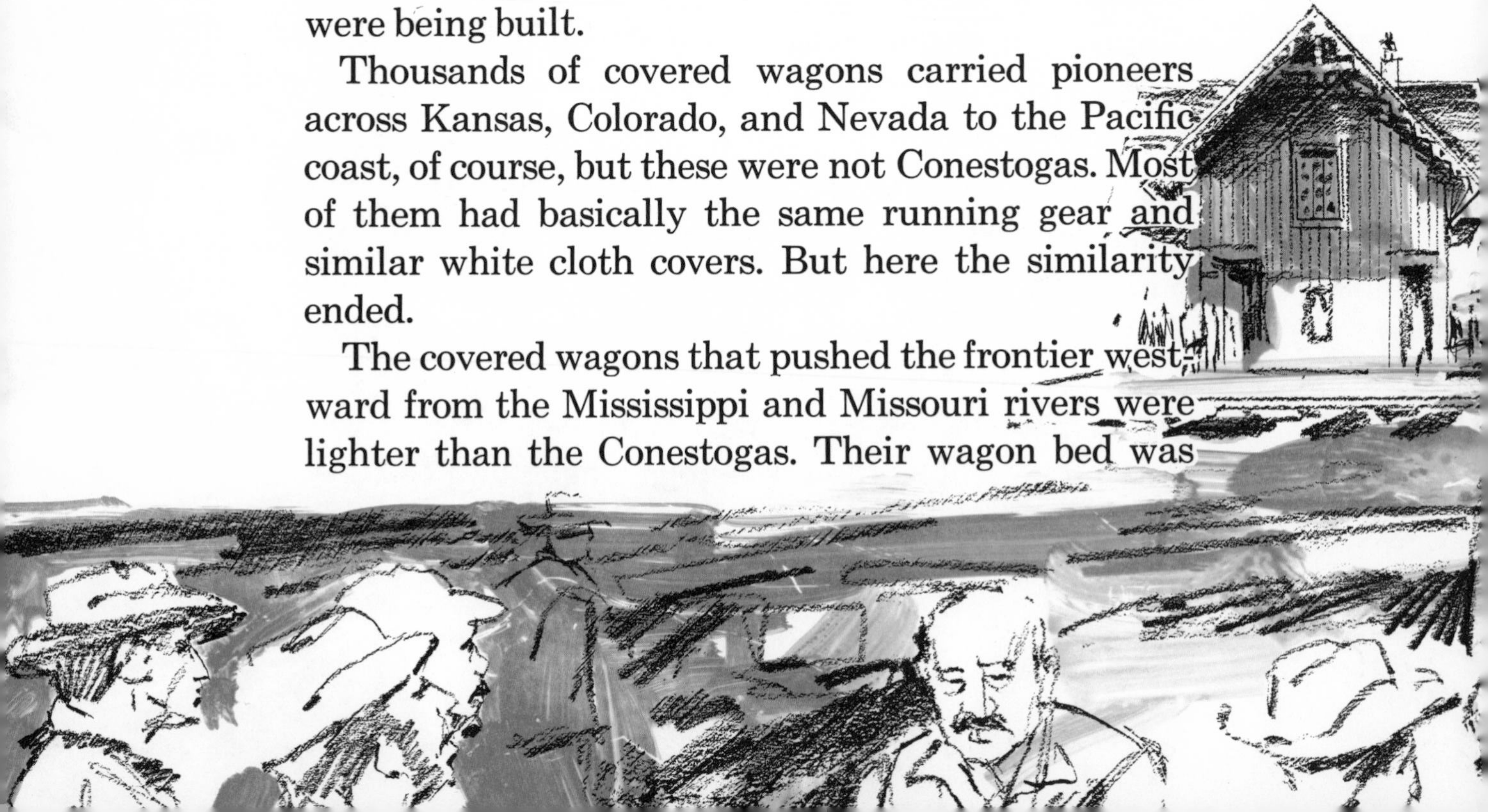

shallow and flat-bottomed, and the ends were squared. Most of them had a driver's seat and the animals were controlled by reins instead of a single "jerk-line." They were not as beautiful as the Conestoga, but they, too, earned a place in American history.

Now the settlers came from the East by boat or train as far as Missouri. Here they bought their wagons, animals and provisions for their journey to the frontier and beyond. The wagons they purchased were built in the Middle West. The builders were not the fine craftsmen who had made the Conestogas. These were practical men who could not spend the extra time to make a gracefully curved wagon bed. With thousands of pioneers pouring in from the East every month, they had to build wagons quickly.

Even before the start of the Civil War, the story of the Conestoga wagon had ended. They had given way to progress made in roads, railroads, canals, and newer wagons. A few of the gracious old wagons remain today in museums, mostly in the East where they were made. They are relics of a glorious era in American history.

In the days when only rutted, rock-strewn trails wound through the mountain barrier, the big, graceful Conestogas played an important part in bringing freedom to Americans to move westward.

About the author: Kenneth G. Richards, a New Englander by birth, developed an early interest in American history. He retired from the U.S. Navy in 1966 and is following a writing career begun during his military service. He is the author of ten books in the PEOPLE OF DESTINY series, and has written many magazine articles. In 1963, Freedoms Foundation at Valley Forge awarded him the George Washington Honor Medal for a magazine article on the *Gettysburg Address*. Mr. Richards now lives in Pacific Grove, California, with his wife and four children.

About the illustrator: James G. Temple has come to Chicago from Alabama by way of Los Angeles and Pittsburgh. He earned his Master of Fine Arts degree from the Art Center College of Design in Los Angeles, and went to Pitt Studios in Pittsburgh for one year. Then he joined a group of free-lance illustrators in Chicago for a year before opening his own studio. James is married and the father of a three-year-old son.